JACOB'S
TROUBLES
A Guide in Parenting

Rosenir Geraci, LCSW-C

Copyright © Year 2025

All Rights Reserved by **Rosenir Geraci, LCSW-C.**

No part of this publication may be reproduced in any form, or by any means, electronic or mechanical, including photocopying, recording, or any information browsing, storage, or retrieval system, without permission in writing from Rosenir Geraci, LCSW-C.

ISBN

Hardcover: 978-1-969120-13-8
Paperback: 978-1-969120-12-1

Dedication

Dedicated to all parents struggling to raise their children the best way they can.

Acknowledgment

My gratitude to Mary Nedrick for her vision and encouragement for the book.

CONTENTS

Dedication i

Acknowledgment ii

Editor Note: iv

About the Author v

Introduction vi

Chapter 1: Parents' Preferences, Children's Troubles? 1

Chapter 2: Real Love 5

Chapter 3: Consequences-Learning What Is Right 6

Chapter 4: God's Perfect Plan 7

Chapter 5: Protecting The Family 9

Chapter 6: Good Parenting 11

Chapter 7: The Most Precious Commodity 13

Chapter 8: Proper Discipline 15

Chapter 9: Independent Thinking 17

Chapter 10: Seeking God's Guidance 19

Editor Note:

Children, in general, are not involved in their parents' conflict but receive the brunt of the consequences of infidelity, financial problems, unrealistic marriage expectations, and lack of commitment when they occur. Parents will seek therapy for their children's presenting problems without noticing that therapy should start with them. Christians have an average marriage conflict rate that is 35% lower than the average population. Nonetheless, all problems, regardless of their difficulty, can be addressed with sound counseling principles found in God's Word, the Bible. This book gives us an example of this approach.

About the Author

Rosenir Geraci is a Licensed Clinical Social Worker and an Approved Drug and Alcohol Supervisor, with 25 years of experience in providing mental health services in the State of Maryland and the State of Florida. Rosenir Geraci was the founder and director of Total Health Resources, Inc., and the former director of the Children's Department at The Center for Mental Health in Washington, DC. Currently, she provides online mental health services for patients around the country. She has extensive experience in providing clinical evaluations, diagnostic reports, and psychotherapy services for individuals, families, couples, adolescents, and children with diverse diagnoses. Her mental health approach is complemented by a Christian perspective to encourage those who believe in Christ to be even better parents, strengthening the families.

Introduction

Whenever we mention Jacob's trouble, we think about the all-night struggle Jacob had with the angel of the Lord by the Jabbok River. Even though the troubles Jacob faced in that all-night fight were excruciating, the root of Jacob's troubles started way before that. It was the culmination of a long history of jealousy between brothers and the favoritism demonstrated by their parents. I think I will not be stretching too much if I say that the root of Jacob's troubles started with the parenting skills of his mother and father.

How much do good or bad parenting skills have to do with the outcome of a child's life?

This is true in almost all cases of child troubles. When a child is brought up for therapy, we can easily evaluate that there is no child with problems; there are parents with problems.

Chapter 1: Parents' Preferences, Children's Troubles?

Scripture describes two children, Jacob and Esau, with very different personalities, a phenomenon that often occurs in families. Those of you who have more than one child know very well that each one has a unique personality, very different from the others. Scripture also describes how Jacob and Esau's parents had their preferences in accordance with their likings. Apparently, this went on throughout their growing-up years. Way before the trick played on the elderly Isaac, the differences in the character of the two children were evident by Esau hastily exchanged his birthright, which involved not only material but especially spiritual blessings, for a bowl of soup that Jacob had diligently prepared, without a second thought.

Isaac and Rebecca not only took preference but also established a clear line of defense for their preferred one.

Discover what you may not like in the character of one of your children and see if it is a reflection of a limitation of your own character.

We as parents, quite often, dislike seeing our defects mirrored back to us in our children's behavior. We do not see the connection between the child's defects and our own defects.

Ironically, we have the tendency not to accept, and even to reject, the child who is the most similar to ourselves. On the other hand, we tend to admire and encourage certain of the favored child's qualities that we lack and would love to have.

The parents went to the ultimate length to make sure that their preferred one would have the upper hand: Isaac knew that Jacob was the divinely appointed heir of God's blessings, but Esau, was a hunter, strong, impulsive, and adventurous, qualities Isaac admired and would like to have himself, which made Esau his preferred child. The angel of the Lord had said, "The older will serve the younger," but Isaac insisted on blessing Esau according to the Israelite tradition.

Rebecca, on the other hand, had no limits in trying to secure the blessings for her preferred child, even by her own power. Right there, I dare say, in the very preferences of the parents, Jacob's troubles started. Issac indulged Esau, and Rebecca overprotected Jacob. In Fundamentals of Christian Education, Ellen White counsels against both extremes; "Mistaken parents … think that by gratifying the wishes of their children, and letting them follow their own inclinations, they can gain their love. What an error! Children thus indulged grow up unrestrained in their desires, unyielding in their dispositions, selfish, exacting, and overbearing, a curse to themselves and to all around them."

We as parents, quite often, dislike seeing our defects mirrored back to us in our children's behavior. We do not like to see the connection between the child's defects and our own defects.

Ironically, we have the tendency not to accept, even to reject, the child that is most like ourselves. On the other hand, we tend to admire and encourage certain qualities of the child that we lack and would love to have. Issac had been himself the only child in his family, he probably was (and the scriptures give some indication) … overprotected. Issac may have been a momma's boy himself and because of this, admired the independence and adventurous character of Esau, and did not appreciate the "hanging-around-mother" qualities of Jacob.

Rebecca, on the other hand, had no limits in trying to secure the blessings for her preferred child, Jacob, the quiet, reserved, spiritual child, even if it meant using her own power. Rebecca, nonetheless, by devising and implementing the plan that granted her desires, showed some level of boldness, impulsiveness, and impatience, much like Esau, the one who reflected her own qualities. In her estimate, Esau did not deserve the powerful blessings. The mirror that our children provide is excellent to make us conscious of our defects. Ironically, parents often say, when they see something they don't like in their children's character: You are just like your father, or just like your mother. Not always… chances are they are just like us. We need to carefully and impartially study our children's characters, including their qualities and defects, and honestly examine ourselves, not only to improve the children's character but also to improve our own character.

Use the mirror our children provide to improve ourselves

"If parents would take up their God-given work and would teach self-restraint, self-denial, and self-control to their children, both by precept and example, they would find that while they were seeking to do their duty, so as to meet the approval of God, they would be learning precious lessons in the school of Christ. They would be learning patience, forbearance, love, and meekness, and these are the very lessons that they must teach to their children." (**EW- The Parents work Pacific Health Journal, January 1890)**

Chapter 2:
Real Love

In educating children, impatience, arrogance, tyranny, but especially indulgence, reflect a deep lack of real love for them often times, not consciously, but out of ignorance of what love is all about. Real love includes discipline, fostering self-sufficiency, and independence. Lack of real love instills in our children *rebellion*, which is a lack of respect for God, and *deception*, which is a lack of respect for men. Parenting is the most important job we have; we are partners with God in molding our children's characters. The proper discipline for children and for parents will help parents to achieve the highest goal of children's education, which is to prepare them to be good servants of God and good servants of their fellow men. Thus, being prepared to become citizens of Heaven.

Each generation is to draw closer to God until there is a generation that reflects the character of Christ and is ready for the Day of Atonement.

"Character building is the most important work ever entrusted to human beings, and never before was its diligent work so important as now. Never was any previous generation called to meet issues so momentous; never before were young men and women confronted by perils so great as confront them today." (**EW - Sign of the Times, September 1894**)

Chapter 3: Consequences-Learning What Is Right

When parents fail in their job, the Lord, in His infinite mercy, steps in to undo what poor parenting skills have developed in a child's character. God's discipline comes to the rescue. However, we do not always accept God's discipline as we should. We do not always see its regenerative intention. Because we do not like to see our children suffering… The discipline of God is difficult to accept.

However, God's discipline never fails. After Jacob departed from his home, he was tricked many times by Laban, his father-in-law, and even by his own children, to become conscious and learn the painful consequences of treachery, especially from close relatives. **In the book Desires of Ages, pg. 301, (E.W.) we read:**

"Through afflictions, God reveals to us the plagued spots of our characters, that by His grace, we may overcome our faults."

Chapter 4: God's Perfect Plan

The family is God's perfect plan to provide an environment and the conditions most appropriate for our development. Within the close relationships of a family, we have the opportunity to test our defects. At the same time, we have the perfect opportunity to develop qualities that would be difficult to develop otherwise. For example, it is easier to become unselfish and patient with those we love and are our own flesh than with strangers.

Why is it such a concern for our development? Why did the Lord carefully design such a developmental tool as a family? What is the purpose of all of this? What is the purpose of life? I will give you my definition: The purpose of life is to glorify God on earth.

"May your will be done here on earth, as it is in Heaven."

How can we do that? What does it mean to "glorify God on earth"? Well, when our children accomplish good things or behave in a good way, everybody who sees it comments, "Hum… the parents did a good job educating this child." Isn't that right? The parents are glorified by the child behavior. In the same way, we glorify God's name on earth by learning, with God's mercy, to curb our defects and further develop qualities given to us by God Himself.

The family is God's perfect designed tool for the

development of our qualities, and the curbing of our defects in the context of love.

Chapter 5: Protecting The Family

It is no wonder that we have the current attack on the family. The Devil is bent on destroying it. Today, we learn in colleges and universities that what we call 'family' can be any number of relationships. Our Lord knew what a family should be. For our own good… a man, a woman, and their children, under God's guidance. A child needs the strengths that only a man and a woman can give. However, when a father is missing, a grandfather or even an uncle can fill the gap. In the same manner, when a mother is missing, a grandmother or aunt will supply that need. The child needs male and female role models.

Often, the love of mothers is unconditional. Her child may become a criminal, and she will still say he or she is my child. The fathers are more conditional; If you behave as I tell you, you are my child, but if you do not, you are not. In this, there is balance. God is our example: He has both conditional and unconditional love for us.

John 14:21 says, *"He that has my commandments, and keeps them, he it is that loves me; and he that loves me shall be loved of my father, and I will love him, and manifest myself to him."*

Rom 5:8 mentions, *"But God commanded his love to us that while we were yet sinners, Christ died for us."*

We as Christians have a high rate of divorce, which is a tragedy for the family and for society. However, we have an even higher rate of marriages having all kinds of abuse: verbal, physical, sexual, and emotional, which ends up being the defining influence of the children's development. Unfortunately, these forms of abuse are true within the so-called Christian homes. I say the "so-called" because if it were indeed Christian homes… this should never occur. I have seen many mothers who failed to defend their daughters, and even sometimes their sons, from their father's abuse. Many spouses, and I say spouses, because wives and husbands, are exposed for years to verbal and even physical abuse witnessed by their children.

Sometimes, the abuse is extended to the children themselves. The abused spouses justify themselves with: "I can't divorce him/her because I am a Christian," and with this, they allow the abuse to go on and on, sometimes for years. Our Lord never condones or justifies any kind of abuse. As parents, our foremost obligation is to protect those who depend on us for their safety; whatever is necessary to be done must be done. Above all, the abuse must come to an end.

"Love God above all, and love others as you love yourselves" is the command.

Chapter 6: Good Parenting

"The will of God is the law of Heaven... As long as God's law is revealed in our earthly homes, the family will be happy." (EW **Ellen White in Child Guidance pg. 74.**)

That being said, we then understand that good parenting has two fundamental aspects: First, seeking God's will or submitting to his authority and guidance. Second: dedicating time to our children to get to know and study their characters, helping them to develop for God's glory. It is not an easy task, especially when you have more than one child, each one with their specific tendencies.

Some years ago, the idea of parents spending "quality time" with their children became quite popular. The premise was that it is not so important how much time is spent with the children, but rather the quality of the time spent with them. That justified and pacified many very busy parents.

However, today, it is worse. We see parents spending their "quality time" focusing on the internet, on Facebook, or on their iPhones, while "being" with their children, during the short time they have "to be" with their children. In reality, their body is with the children, but they are not THERE! Parents need to be there and have the children as the focus of their attention. It is the only way parents can get to really know their children and themselves.

I cannot tell you how many children have complained to

me in my office (sometimes very young ones): "My mother does not pay attention to me, she only pays attention to her cell phone, when I talk to her, she says, "Hum… hum… but I know she is not listening." The children feel, and often verbalize to me, that they feel abandoned. No amount of goods, games, and even books with which parents try to compensate for the lack of presence in their lives can make up for their support, love, and example. Time is the most precious commodity in life. In everything that is important to us in life, we invest time: our careers, our relationships, our possessions.

So, time is one of the most important gifts we can give to our children. However, our society has encouraged multitasking as a quality to the point of causing us to ask: Is it really multitasking, or is it a neurosis? Have you noticed that when we watch the news on TV, we have a multilayered display of information: we have the speaker, and then under the image, we have other news being displayed, followed by the weather in another line, and sometimes even the day's stock market information in another line. As a result, no information receives the attention it deserves, and everything appears superficial. It really trains the viewer to lack concentration, rendering them unable to think in depth about anything; in summary, it makes them a neurotic person.

Chapter 7:
The Most Precious Commodity

"Many parents plead that they have so much to do that they have no time to improve their minds, to educate their children for practical life, or to teach them how they may become lambs of Christ's fold. Parents must not neglect to arm their own minds against sin, to guard against that which will not only ruin themselves but transmit pain and every kind of misery and evil to their offspring." **Ellen White continues in Child Guidance Pg. 75**

By the time Jesus turned 12, he had already marveled the doctors of the law with his profound knowledge and understanding of the scriptures. Certainly, his mother invested considerable time in teaching him the precious truth. Obviously, she herself knew the scriptures well in order to teach him.

In the initial years that Moses spent in his Hebrew home, he learned moral principles that he never forgot, not even with the years he spent in the Egyptian court. Daniel learned physical, intellectual, and moral principles in his growing-up years, which sustained and protected him in the many years of service in the heathen courts. Not to mention Joseph, the list goes on and on, to show us the importance of parents who seek the Lord themselves and apply all that they learn in the education of their children, with attention and dedication, not in an aggressive, impatient, hurried, or casual manner.

Take time to know God, to know yourself, and to know your

children

It is only by truly knowing God that we can understand His will and wishes for us. We also need to know ourselves, including our qualities, limitations, and faults. Additionally, it is important to understand our children and their potential. We must recognize both their inherited and acquired faults. This understanding allows us to discipline them appropriately. The goal of discipline should be to promote their development. We, parents, need to develop in our characters the fruit of the Spirit: love, joy, peace, patience, kindness, goodness, faithfulness, gentleness, and above all, self-control to impart proper discipline.

Chapter 8: Proper Discipline

Had Isaac and Rebecca set the appropriate boundaries for their children, maybe Esau would have learned not to be so impulsive. Instead of being corrected, he was loved and admired by his father for this character trait.. Maybe he would have learned to reflect on the consequences before acting. This would have saved him from the loss and remorse of selling his birthright for a bowl of porridge. Perhaps Esau would have learned one of the most valuable secrets of life: To delay gratification.

As a Christian psychiatrist, Scott Peck, said, "To learn to delay gratification is to learn to schedule the pain and pleasures of life in such a way as to enhance the pleasure by meeting and experiencing the pain first and getting it over with. "This is, most of the time, a process that we learn naturally in life. We learn early in life that it is better to wait to eat our dessert after we first eat dinner that we don't like it so much. We learn that if we go for sweets on an empty stomach, we may end up with very upsetting consequences. However, more and more, this is a vital quality that our society no longer gives importance to.

Today, this is one of the greatest pitfalls our children must face. Many youths today, since early childhood, have been indulged like Esau, to know that their desires have to be satisfied "Right now," with terrible consequences for their characters. Many adolescents cannot wait for sex, or for going through the struggles of building a successful career, or for developing an independent life. I have seen depressed fathers and mothers at 15 and 14 years old. They could not wait to become adults to develop responsible parenthood. I often see middle and high school kids who state that they need to "enjoy life" because they are young, and this is the purpose of youth. They do not have time to spend in "boring" and "limiting" schools, so they skip classes and prefer to attend skipping parties, where drugs, alcohol, and sex are free and abundant. This is what they call "enjoying life." Many adolescents develop the wrong notion that they are entitled to independence just because they have grown up, not because they have developed an independent life. Their parents have failed to teach them, by discipline and example, to delay gratification.

Certainly, if Esau had learned to delay gratification, he would not have felt as many adolescents now feel, that "they will die, right then and there," if they don't get what they want.

Chapter 9: Independent Thinking

As for Jacob, he was thoughtful and quiet, but he did not appear to have independent thinking, probably because he was too much under his mom's control. He was at least 40 years old when his mother approached him with that mischievous plan. How do we know this? The scripture says that about the time that Isaac decided to pour out his blessings, Rebecca was tired of Esau's Canaanite wives. Esau married two Canaanite women when he was 40. Since Esau and Jacob were twins, it is reasonable to assume that Jacob was at least 40 years old by that time.

Nonetheless, despite having doubts about the idea, he still proceeded with it. He offered a mild, flimsy doubt. He could have at least discussed the matter with his mother. s Jacob was well-versed in the scriptures, but he did not reason with his mother that deceiving the father was not the right thing to do. He simply stated, "My father will curse me, because he will find out that I am not Esau." He questioned the effectiveness of the plan, not the plan itself. When his mother said, for the second time, "Do it as I tell you." This was sufficient for him. Here, there is a word of caution about loving a child so much that we forget that the child is not an extension of ourselves. Even though a child inherits a lot of our personality traits, he or she has her own personality, which needs to be nourished and encouraged. Jacob's lack of questioning could have been the result of such an enmeshing of personalities that he had no opinion of his own. Later in life, he encountered, by God's mercy, many situations that fostered his decision-making capacities. "While children and youth gain knowledge of facts… let them learn to draw lessons and discern truth for themselves." (E.G. Education pg. 119)

As we can see Jacob's trouble by the Jabbok river, had much deeper roots: The consequences of an error in parenting, led to many awful consequences for the entire family. These extended even to the next generation. Isaac suffered tremendously for being tricked. Scripture says Isaac "trembled greatly" when he found out he had been irreversibly tricked. After this trickery, Rebecca never saw her beloved son again, she had passed when her son returned. Jacob in consequence of this, suffered loneliness, treachery, he worked almost as a slave for 14 years…. Not to mention the struggle by the Jabbok River. A struggle were everything Jacob became and owned was at peril; from his conscience to his family life. By God's grace he prevailed and found in this struggle a blessing. It is interesting to see that in every struggle we go through in life, if we hold on to the Lord, we will find a blessing in it. Then the suffering we go through is not in vain.

We would imagine that the consequences of the parents' mistake would end at the Jabbok river, but years later the example Jacob received, he passed on to the next generation as he gave preference to his son Joseph, and indulged Joseph which resulted in grave consequences for Joseph and for himself. Thank God he has a way to transform bad into good for those who love and respect him.

Chapter 10: Seeking God's Guidance

To impart the proper discipline on our children, we need first to know God well, for he offers the best parenting example we can have. If we meditate on how the Lord has dealt with us, we can see clearly how to deal with our children. We can clearly see his love towards us in the way he forgave, rewarded, praised, and sometimes punished us. If we look deep into his punishments, we see that they are never to humiliate or destroy us, but to encourage, change, and develop us. Unfortunately, in setting boundaries, parents often vent their frustrations or worries about appearances. Parents often forget that they are in place of God for their children, and therefore, the guidance parents provide should always be guided by love and above all by EXAMPLE.

The parenting process parallels the sanctification process very well: it is the work of a lifetime. We have to be committed despite the setbacks. The children grow up to become our friends, and as such, they often need a word of guidance from more experienced adults… Don't give up! Day by day, if you are faithful, the Lord has promised:

"Train the child the way he should go, and when they grow up, they will not depart from it."

Shall the prey be taken from the mighty,

Or the captives of the righteous be delivered?

But thus says the LORD:

"Even the captives of the mighty shall be taken away,

And the prey of the terrible be delivered;

For I will contend with him who contends with you,

And I will save your children. (Isaiah 49:24,25)

The father of the fatherless and a defender of widows is God in his holy dwelling. In Psalm 68:5

There is a beautiful poem from Khalil Gibran that reminds us: (The parentheses are mine)

Your children are not your children…

They are the sons and daughters of life(God)

Longing for itself (Him).

They come through you, but they are not from you

Though they are with you,

They belong not to you.

May God help each one of us to be committed to the saving of our children, to submit to the leading of God in their education, and one day, when God asks: Where is the flock that was given thee? Thy beautiful flock? We may present them back in the beauty of holiness, to him that entrusted them to us.